Teenage Refugees From

SOMALIA

Speak Out

IN THEIR OWN VOICES

Teenage Refugees From

SOMALIA

Speak Out

IKRAM HUSSEIN

GLOBE FEARON EDUCATIONAL PUBLISHER
A Division of Simon & Schuster
Upper Saddle River, New Jersey

Published in 1997 by The Rosen Publishing Group, Inc.
29 East 21st Street, New York, N Y 10010

First Edition
Copyright © 1997 by The Rosen Publishing Group, Inc.

Manufactured in the United States of America.

ISBN 0-835-92231-6

Contents

Introduction   7

1) Ayan: Long Journey to the United States   19

2) Ali: I Want to Start My Life Again   25

3) Nacima: I Will Never Forget My Culture   31

4) Amina: Peace Will Never Come to

     My Country   37

5) Mohamud: There Were Good Times   43

6) Nimco: I Am Not Homesick Anymore   49

7) Abdi: The Simpler Things in Life   55

Glossary   60

For Further Reading   62

Index   63

A starving Somali mother and child in the capital, Mogadishu. The city was the scene of much fighting in Somalia's civil war.

INTRODUCTION

S omalia is located in the Horn of Africa. It is north of Kenya and east of Ethiopia. Djibouti lies in the northeast. The Gulf of Aden is to the north, while the Indian Ocean is on Somalia's eastern coast. Somalia has long been considered an important trade nation. In the past, the towns on Somalia's coast traded with several Arab countries and other Indian Ocean peoples. Arabs traveled to Somalia to buy incense, wood, and ivory. Somalia was known as "God's Land."

From approximately 100 AD to 500 AD, Somalis traded with Egyptian, Phoenician, Persian, Greek, and Roman traders. By the tenth century, Chinese merchants traveled to Somalia to buy giraffes, leopards, and tortoises.

7

During the tenth century, the Islamic faith was introduced in Somalia. Most Somalis today practice Islam. Somali society is also centered around clans. Clans have always been a part of Somali life. A clan is a large group of people who are related to one another by a common ancestor. The clans of Somalia are very similar in terms of culture and religion. They practice Islam and speak the same language. Historically Somalis have had conflicts between clans. But through it all, they have been able to preserve their national unity.

In 1869, the Suez Canal was opened in northern Egypt, opening eastern Africa to Europe. This encouraged Europeans to expand into the region. By 1885, Somalis were living under the colonial rule of three foreign powers: Great Britain, Italy, and France.

These European colonial powers created the borders of present-day Somalia. In the process, large numbers of Somalis were cut off from their clans and forced to live in surrounding nations. Today about 3 million Somalis live in eastern Ethiopia and northern Kenya. Even now the presence of Somalis living outside the country's national borders creates a problem in the region.

Northern Somalia gained its independence from Great Britain in June 1960. Southern Somalia was able to win its independence from Italy one month later. The two areas merged to form the Somali Republic. The Ogaden region to the northwest was first colonized by Italy and then placed under the control of Ethiopia. The new Somali nation was formed during an era of democracy. Clan and regional differences were worked out through multiparty elections.

However, after its independence, Somalia still faced difficult new challenges. The country continued to depend on the Italians and British for economic support. The Somali government borrowed money to build roads, create farms, and improve livestock programs. One of the greatest challenges during this time period was getting Somalis to live peacefully side by side as a nation—not as competing clans.

The Somali government's main goal was to unite all of the areas where Somalis lived into one country. The Somali government also tried to distance itself from its colonial past. It developed foreign relations with the Soviet Union and Eastern Europe. The country began to rebuild slowly.

By the late 1960s, however, the Somali government was seen as inefficient and corrupt. Progress was moving too slowly for the Somali people. They felt their government was improving relations with Ethiopia instead of reclaiming the Ogaden region. Many Somalis were angry.

In October 1969 President Abdirashiid Ali Shermaarke was assassinated. Muhammad Siyad Barre came to power in his place. He ruled the

Gacmo wadajiraa galladi ka dhalataa

ENGLISH TRANSLATION FROM SOMALIAN:
Joined hands bear success.

country for twenty-one years, until the beginning of 1991, when he was overthrown.

Barre changed Somalia dramatically. He got rid of the National Assembly (similar to the U.S. Congress), suspended the country's constitution, and prohibited any form of political gathering. Barre also removed traditional Somali rulers. He then took away clan water and grazing rights. He outlawed the Islamic practice of paying *diya. Diya* is money paid by a person who has injured or killed another person. Barre was attempting to break down the traditional sources of power. He weakened the role of religious leaders and strengthened his own power by creating a dictatorship.

Barre maintained power by suppressing critics, jailing opponents, and encouraging clan rivalries. He also bribed opposition groups to win their support.

In 1976, Barre started a war against Ethiopia. His aim was to regain the Ogaden territory, an area where many people of Somali descent lived. The war ended in 1978. The Somalis were defeated. Approximately 60,000 men died, many soldiers returned home wounded, and about 650,000 Ethiopian refugees of Somali descent fled to Somalia.

During the war, the Soviet Union had supported the Ethiopians. Somalia turned to the United States for military aid. The United States agreed to help arm and train Somali troops. In return, the United States was granted permission to use Somali ports and airfields in the event of a crisis. The Somali armed forces grew much larger. This growth devastated the Somali economy, because a large portion of the national budget went to the military.

Somalia then had to depend on aid from other countries for its economic survival. The Ogaden war created unrest among the people. Somalis realized that the war had not been a good idea, and they began to distrust the government. Opposition groups began to emerge. Barre jailed, tortured, and at times executed people whom he believed opposed him.

Meanwhile, from 1978 to 1979, the region suffered a severe drought, the cost of living skyrocketed, and people could not afford to buy food or fuel. Somalis grew desperate. By the late 1980s it had become clear to many Somalis that Barre had neither the skills nor the vision to lead the country out of its crisis.

Groups opposed to Barre's government began to form outside of the country. One of them was called the Somali National Movement or the SNM. The SNM formed in London in 1981 and then moved to Ethiopia.

In 1988, the SNM attacked Somali government troops in the cities of Hargeisa and Buroa in northern Somalia. Barre's government forces fought back. Many civilians were injured or killed. Others fled their homes and became refugees in Ethiopia. Barre's brutal response to the attack revealed the violent policies of Somalia's government rule. International support for Barre and foreign aid to Somalia began to decrease.

The government attempted to reform some policies because of increasing pressure. The government reintroduced a multiparty system, adopted a new constitution, and called for elections. However, the opposition groups continued to fight. By the end of December 1990, another opposition group, the United Somali Congress (USC) emerged and the conflict spread to the capital, Mogadishu.

In January 1991, Barre's government was overthrown. Following Barre's defeat, the worst

Major General Muhammad Siyad Barre was the president of Somalia for twenty-one years. He maintained a dictatorship over the Somali people. He was overthrown in 1991.

U.S. soldiers arrived in Somalia in 1992 as part of Operation Restore Hope, an American effort to reduce the level of violence and to provide humanitarian aid.

period in modern Somalia's history began. In 1991 and 1992, 40,000 Somalis died in fighting between competing factions.

The government became the enemy of the nation. Thousands of people died daily in the civil war. Civilians were robbed and murdered. No place in Somalia was safe. Many homes had no telephones or electricity. In many cases, people had no idea if relatives living on the other side of the city were dead or alive.

At first the world community ignored what was happening in Somalia. Somali intellectuals living outside the country pleaded with the world community to recognize the human rights abuses that **14** were taking place.

In early 1991, a number of unsuccessful cease-fire attempts were made. Outside parties, such as the Organization of African Unity, the Organization of the Islamic Conference, and the United Nations (UN), failed to stop the fighting in the capital city, Mogadishu. Overall conditions in the country worsened. A severe drought also hit central and southern Somalia that year. Meanwhile, different clans continued to compete for power.

Mogadishu and much of southern and central Somalia slid into chaos. In the absence of any recognized government, power and food were in the hands of those with guns. At least 45 percent of the population fled the violence, drought, and famine in Somalia.

By 1992, one-fourth of the people of Somalia were estimated to be in danger of starvation. In 1993 a relief organization estimated that half of all Somali children under five years of age had died of starvation.

Many farmers could not leave their homes to work on their farms. Armed bandits, under the authority of local warlords, looted houses and stole food shipments. This made the problems of malnutrition and starvation among the Somali people worsen. By this point, many Somalis kept guns in their homes to protect themselves.

In February 1992 the UN and the Organization of African Unity helped bring about a cease-fire. Many countries sent troops to Somalia to aid in the peace process. The world turned its attention to Somalia.

The United States began Operation Provide Relief in August 1992. The United States airlifted emergency supplies into Somalia from Kenya. This was followed in December 1992 by the U.S.-led mission called Operation Restore Hope. The goals were to reduce the level of violence through limited military actions and help the delivery of humanitarian aid. On May 1, 1993, the UN took over command. Starvation has ended, agricultural production has partly recovered, and hostilities have ceased in many parts of Somalia except Mogadishu. The United States and the UN were more successful in preventing widespread famine than in bringing order to Somalia. When the last UN troops pulled out of Somalia in March 1995, Mogadishu still did not have a functioning government.

The northern part of Somalia has seceded (broken away from) the rest of Somalia and is attempting to stabilize its government, even though the international community has not recognized it as a separate country. The new government has been able to provide the people with some basic services and security. Somalis who returned to their homes in the north after the war found mines in their houses and the remains of destroyed water pipes and electrical cables in the streets. Conflicts between clans continue to flare up, and severe shortages make it difficult for Somalis to rebuild their lives.

In the south, fighting between rival clans continues. In the midst of political crisis, no stable government has emerged to provide basic services such as education, security, health care, and transportation.

Thousands of Somali refugees have left their homes because of the civil war. Many are teenage refugees who face fear, confusion, and violence. All of these factors influence how well they adjust in a new environment. Some teenage refugees may not attend school for many years. Others end up taking care of their younger brothers and sisters after their parents have died in war. Only some refugees find happiness and a safe home.

This book presents the stories of several Somali teenage refugees. It describes their journeys as they left their country and came to North America. Their stories show their hopes and dreams for the future.◆

Ayan is seventeen years old. When she left Somalia, she went to several countries in search of a new home. Finally, she came to Buffalo, New York, in 1993. She now enjoys the safety and freedom she has in the United States.

AYAN
LONG JOURNEY TO THE UNITED STATES

I was born in Mogadishu. I lived there all my life until my family left. Before the civil war, my life was normal. I went to school and lived with my family.

I left Somalia in 1991 with my mother and younger brother. We left because of the civil war. We were afraid for our lives. Somalia was not safe. Gangs would break into houses during the night. They would either rob or kill civilians, most of whom had no weapons. It was common to see dead people lying in the streets of Mogadishu.

Such tragic events were unusual for Somalia in the past. It had always been a safe country. The war had a serious effect on me personally

Somalis wait to receive food and water during the civil war.

because I lost some of my classmates in the fighting. They were with their families and planned to get out of the city until the tensions eased. But they never made it out. They were killed before they could leave.

During this time I was worried about every-thing. It was difficult to leave the house.

One day my mother decided that we had to leave Somalia. Even though it was hard for us to leave, we knew we had to do it. I was afraid that we were all going to die. We left all my relatives behind—uncles, aunts, and grandmother. On our way out of Somalia, we stayed at several places in the country: first Qoryoley, then Kismayu. Wherever we went we saw violence and war. Finally we left the country and went to a refugee camp in Kenya. The United Nations helped us to resettle and register in the camp.

I was unhappy for the first few days. The camp was very hot and overcrowded. It was diffi-cult to get water or food. We had to stand in a long line for many hours. Also, the camp was not safe. After the camp officials left for the day, it was easy for women to be robbed or raped. I couldn't wait to leave this camp. Finally, at the end of 1993 I left Kenya for the United States.

Before I came here, I thought living in the United States would be easy. I thought there would be no difficulty in buying whatever I want-ed. But I soon realized this was not true. I found that, just like in Somalia, people here must work hard to achieve anything. I also realized that life here is very different from life in my country. I had to adapt to a new culture. I had to make sense of American culture and the English language. Now that I have adapted, I feel safer and happier being here.

I know I've got to work hard to be successful in this country. I never imagined all it would take. There are so many opportunities in the United States.

When I left my country, I was twelve. I did not go to school for the two years that I lived in the refugee camp. When I started school here, I had to take English classes. Learning English was hard. At the beginning, it was scary to learn another language. I didn't believe I would ever master it.

Schools are different here. Now I am doing well in school. I hope to go to college and someday be a doctor. I believe I have the hope and courage to be successful in the future.

When I first came here, I was very confused. I was surprised to see a Somali person waiting for me at the airport. He was the case worker assigned to me.

In the beginning it was hard to find my way around. Most of the time I didn't know what I was doing or where I was going. Now when I look back, I laugh. I think it is funny.

I have made many friends since I have been here. I like them all. Many of them are nice and helpful. In my free time I like to hang out with them. Sometimes we play soccer. When I am alone, I like to write in my diary. I want my friends to know about my culture. I want them to respect the way I do certain things. I hope they will understand these differences and realize my background is very different from theirs. I went through some frightening experiences before coming here.

I hope the fighting will stop in Somalia and peace will come. I hope people will resolve their differences and try to take care of each other.

I want to help my country in the future. Someday I will visit it when these problems are worked out. I can't forget my country.◆

Ali has had many terrible experiences in his young life. Both of his parents and one of his sisters were killed in the violence in Somalia. At eighteen, he knows what it is like to be homeless and in danger. After arriving very recently in North America, Ali is focusing on his future and on rebuilding his shattered life.

2
ALI
I WANT TO START MY LIFE AGAIN

I am eighteen years old and have been in the United States for three days. Everything is very new to me, and I am sad all the time. I am on my way to Canada to stay with my older sister and her family. It has taken me five years to get to Canada. I have been to Ethiopia, Kenya, UAE (United Arab Emirates), and Holland before coming here. I am tired of traveling, especially because I cannot stay anywhere I go. Sometimes it is because the people I am with cannot keep me; sometimes the government of that country does not want me. I want to go someplace where I can settle in peace and have the opportunity to live a good life.

This photo of a Mogadishu street in the 1950s shows evidence of the Italian presence in Somalia. Somalia achieved independence from Italy in 1960.

Until 1991 I lived in Baidoa with my three sisters and my parents. Baidoa was a beautiful place. My father was a tailor, and my mother helped him. The business was enough to support us. I had a bicycle and my sisters had nice clothes. Then the clans began fighting, and my father was killed by members of another clan. Some men took him away from his shop, and two days later our relatives found his body. We could not even bury him—the situation in the town was too dangerous.

My mother took us to hide with relatives on the outskirts of town for about a month. We hoped to go back to our town, but then we heard that my father's shop had been looted and that our house had been taken by other people who would kill us if we came back. We realized that we had to run for our lives, so we began the long journey to Ethiopia. This was the worst experience of my life. On the second day, our bus was attacked by bandits who killed many people and raped my mother and many other women. My mother and my sister Jamilla were killed, and I was separated from my other two sisters, Fatima and Amina. I escaped by hiding in some bushes with some men. We had to walk for four days to get to Ethiopia. Finally, two weeks later, we reached a refugee camp.

The refugee camp was very crowded, and I saw many people I knew. Everybody was in bad shape because they had lost members of their families and had terrible experiences getting to the camp. When I saw people I knew, I would cry as I thought of my family, especially my mother. But life in the camp was okay. There was water, food, and even a school. I started to make some friends, but I was still very sad and missed my two sisters who had disappeared. Four months later I heard that my sisters were in Kismayu, a town in southern Somalia, so I arranged with an uncle to go there to meet them. This was a long trip, but nothing happened to us, and I was able to find my sisters. It was good to see them, but it also made me sad because it made me think of my parents.

Women in Afgoi, Somalia, dig for grass to sell as food. One million Somalis were in danger of starvation in 1991.

We stayed in Kismayu for more than two years. My older sister Fatima went to Kenya because there was a possibility of going to the United States from there. We had all heard good things about the United States and were very excited about it. Fatima went to a refugee camp, and a few months later she was taken to the United States. Since we did not have parents or any adults to help us, Fatima told me to wait until I was older and then I would be able to join her. My sister Amina went to the camp in Kenya the next year and from there she went to the United States, too.

My father's brother arranged for me to go to the United Arab Emirates, where he was working.

I stayed there for two years. I was able to go to school and learn English. Then my uncle lost his job and I had to leave because the government would not let us stay. I was able to get a refugee visa to Holland. My sisters sent me money to go there; in the meantime, they tried to get me a visa to come to the United States. I stayed in Holland for seven months. It was quite nice there. There were a lot of Somalis in Holland, and the Dutch government was very generous with educational assistance and money. Many people in Holland did not like African refugees, however, and sometimes this made me uncomfortable.

My sisters have told me to go to Canada instead of joining them in the United States. They say that there are better opportunities for me in Canada. My sisters live in St. Louis, Missouri, and they say that it is hard for the Somalis who live there to go to school because the government is not very helpful. I hope that when I go to Canada the people will not discriminate against me because I am a refugee.

There are many Somalis in Canada, including my relatives, who can help me. Maybe one day I will come back to the United States and have a chance to see things here. Right now, I am excited about starting a life in Canada.◆

Nacima came from Mogadishu, Somalia. She spent three years in refugee camps and on the road. When she left Somalia at age fourteen, she was already very mature. She came to San Diego, California, with her family in 1995. Her memory of Somalia is one of fear. She is glad to be safe at last.

NACIMA
I WILL NEVER FORGET MY CULTURE

I was born in Mogadishu. I was ten years old when I left my country in 1991. I left with my mother, younger sister, and brother.

I didn't know what had happened to my father. When everybody fled from Mogadishu, we lost each other. The last time we saw him was the day before we left. He told my mother that he would catch up with us in Kenya.

My family left Somalia because of the civil war. Our house was robbed many times by army gangs, and four of my uncles were killed in the civil war. We decided to leave because the situation was getting worse. It was dangerous to stay in Mogadishu.

The only way to leave Somalia is to escape

during the middle of the night. My family took a bus from Mogadishu and went to Kismayu. We stayed there until it was no longer safe. It began to feel like no place was safe anymore. Finally we took a boat to Kenya. The trip lasted two weeks. At that time, my mother was nine months pregnant. My youngest brother was born while we were still on the boat. Since my mother could not care for all of us, I had to take care of my younger siblings. It was difficult to travel in the overcrowded boat.

When we came to Kenya, we stayed in a refugee camp near the border. We still didn't know where my father was.

We lived in refugee camps for the next three years. We had many problems at the first camp. Some of the refugees weren't nice to my mother— they knew my father wasn't there to protect us. They fought constantly with her. Our tent was burned down by some people who lived in the camp with us. Later the UN moved us to another camp. We stayed there until we left for the United States.

We had waited for my father in Kenya for three years, but we could not find him. We left Kenya without hearing from him.

I came to San Diego, California, with my family five months ago. Before I arrived, I hoped the United States would be a safe and beautiful place. I like it here because I feel safe. The quality of life is good. The educational system is good, too.

I WONDER WHY!

I am a Somali and some ask why
We stand and watch our people die
I will tell you why we feel hopeless, sometimes useless
Most of all, however, we feel homeless

I am a Somali
I wonder why everything we ever held dear is no longer here
It seems as though it disappeared
I am a Somali and I weep not for me but for what no longer is
and will never be

I am a Somali and I know how
That hatred is the very core
The bitter soul of any war
It is a war that destroyed the whole
Will destroy more and more

Poem by Somali refugee teen

We did not know where my father was until we came here. One day we received a letter from him. In it he explained what had happened and that he was in Kenya. I wish he could be here with us now. I really miss him. My mother is filling out legal papers so he can join us in San Diego. This process might take a long time, though, anywhere from several months to several years.

I attend the same school as my younger sister and brother. It was impossible to go to school in the camps. The last time I went to school was when I was in my country.

Somali children greet U.S. soldiers upon their arrival in Somalia in August 1992.

When I came here, I had difficulty concentrating in class. I had so many things on my mind.

In the beginning I felt uneasy being part of a group I couldn't understand. Some students would tease me and sometimes pick on me. I didn't like that, and I spoke to the teacher when it happened.

Now I like my school. I've been here only a short time, so I still don't understand everything the teacher says. But I like learning. My teacher is nice and helps me when I have a hard time.

I would like my classmates to help me when I don't understand something. I would also like them to know that my life has not been easy for

the past few years.

When we came here, everything was different and confusing. My younger sister and brother were scared to eat the food. My younger sister often had bad dreams. Sometimes I could not remember my address or telephone number. The first few days, I had a hard time finding the school-bus stop.

It is unfortunate that my only memories of Somalia are frightening. The last few months before we left, I remember armed men walking around the city streets, scaring the people away. I also remember that my relatives were scared and worried about what would happen next. I often think about my grandmother. I hope she is okay. I hope she can join us soon.

When I first came here I felt pressure. Being the oldest, I had to help my mother look after my younger siblings. My mother worries about us growing up here. She wants to make sure that we do not forget our culture.◆

Amina is nineteen years old. She is the oldest child in her family. She and her brother came to Canada before the rest of their family. Amina has many friends in Canada and enjoys pursuing several hobbies.

AMINA
PEACE WILL NEVER COME TO MY COUNTRY

I was born in Mogadishu in July 1978. I left Somalia in a rush. I did not have time to say goodbye to my friends. I have been living in Ottawa, Canada, for the past five and a half years.

I left my country during the early stages of the war in Mogadishu. The war was not yet out of control, but by that time the schools were no longer open. When they had been open, government officials came in and harassed the students and teachers. The government also arrested many innocent people daily. Civilians were often accused of wrongdoing. At my school some students were taken away to jail. The government accused them of being part of a religious movement acting against the state. Their only reason

A student helps serve lunch to younger students at a school in Mogadishu. Food was used to encourage pupils to come back to school during the period of widespread starvation in 1993.

for accusing the students was that my school was a parochial school.

Before I left Somalia, the country was going through a difficult time. The cost of living increased; for instance, the price of food rose dramatically. Many people could not afford to meet their basic needs. Everyone feared for their lives.

My family and I experienced a lot of pressure because my father worked for the government. It was common for government workers to be accused of supporting the enemy. At night when we were home, we could hear the sound of gunfire. We heard the noise and didn't know if some of our neighbors were being attacked, but we couldn't help them because we were afraid for our own lives. For all we knew, we could be next. We were never certain what would happen.

When I first came to Canada I was often confused. I missed my family, and I did not understand why my brother and I could not stay with them, no matter how bad the situation. I also felt helpless and guilty for not being there to help them. But I was luckier than many. My brother and other family members were here to give each other support.

Many times I felt like an outsider. Nothing was familiar at all. I thought I would never be able to finish school or get a job. The values here were so different from the ones I learned in Somalia. My first day at school, for instance, I was surprised to see the students not wearing uniforms. The students' attitudes toward the teachers were much different from what I was used to at home. In Somalia we had to respect our teachers. We could never question them in the manner that was allowed in Canada. Somehow it felt like I needed to learn everything all over again.

Learning English was very difficult for me. At first it seemed like an impossible task. It was difficult to start speaking this new language. I always had the feeling that I was doing it wrong. If I had not surrounded myself with English-speaking friends, I don't believe I would know it as well as I do now. Today I speak and understand English very well.

Traditionally, Somalis are a nomadic people who travel with their animals. Only about 30 percent of the population is still nomadic. Camels are especially valuable to the nomads because of their ability to travel long distances with little water.

Before I came to Canada, I was told that it was a place where you lose your faith and culture. After five years of living here, I have to agree that there is some truth to that. When you are new here, it is easy to lose your focus. There are so many distractions. There are, however, some good aspects of Canadian culture, which I have been able to absorb into my own life.

Since I have gotten used to living here, I do enjoy myself and feel more comfortable. I have made many friends over the years. For fun, I like reading, going to the movies, and playing basketball. I like to hang out with my friends and surf the Internet whenever I get the chance.

Now I am studying pre-law. I hope to study international law in the future. I like living in Canada because there are plenty of educational opportunities.

When I think about my country, I cannot stop hoping for peace. I don't think it will come during my lifetime. Unfortunately, I have no hope of my country ever being the same. I don't think I will go back home, as long as the current levels of conflict and economic instability continue. The infrastructure of the country needs to be rebuilt. But even if that happens, I doubt the constant struggle for power between leaders will ever stop.

I wish that no one had to go through the experience of being a refugee. I tell my Canadian friends that they should not take their country's peace for granted. Like someone said, Canada is my home, but Somalia will remain my country.◆

Mohamud, sixteen, is Amina's brother. He wants North Americans to know more about Somalia than what they see on the news. He remembers many happy and peaceful times during his childhood in Somalia.

MOHAMUD
THERE WERE GOOD TIMES

I left my country because it had become un-safe. I have been in Ottawa, Canada, since 1990. I came here with my sister. The rest of my family has remained in Somalia. At the beginning, I was scared that my sister and I would not survive. I also worried about the rest of the family we left behind.

My last few months in Somalia were difficult. I was scared because I was a young man. During the civil war, men were the first ones to be taken to jail. There was a curfew in the city. After sunset everyone was supposed to stay home. My parents always advised me not to go anywhere alone, especially near the end of the day. After school I was expected to go straight home. I could not spend time with my friends. Normally we played soccer after school, but once the civil war started, it became impossible.

Before I came to Canada, I didn't know the geography of North America. I thought Canada was part of the United States! When I first came to Canada, I was not very happy because I had left my family behind. It was hard to communicate. I had a hard time understanding English. It was not easy for me to get used to the way people spoke. But the more I watched television, the better I understood the language.

Currently I am in my last year of high school. Next year when I go to the university I want to study business. I hope someday to own my own company. I like the schools here because it is easier to focus only on subjects of interest. At home I was required to take all subjects. Here I can dedicate my attention to the sciences or liberal arts. In this way I am able to concentrate on my area of interest sooner.

I miss certain things about Somalia, especially the holidays and celebrations, such as Id and Ramadan. These are Muslim holidays. I used to look forward to these holidays when I lived in Somalia. Now when these days come, I feel kind of sad. No one here knows about them. I also miss my home. I miss the feeling of community.

Canada is media-driven. The only thing Canadians know about my country is what they see on television. I want the people here to know that

A refugee woman from Baidoa waits for food in Mogadishu.

In 1958, Somalis marched in the streets of Mogadishu to celebrate their country's upcoming independence from Italy.

my country was not always at war, and that people were not always starving. There were good times when people were happy and lived peacefully together. The current situation in Somalia is the reason refugees came to Canada. In my country's past, there were no Somali refugees.

I like Canada. Here I have the freedom to make whatever I want of my life. There are many opportunities here, but I do miss Somalia very much. I never stop thinking about my country, relatives, school, and friends. I often think about the way my hometown of Mogadishu looked before I left. It is very different from how it is shown on television. I hope the killing stops and efforts to rebuild the country begin. I would like to go back to Somalia when it is safe.◆

Nimco is seventeen years old and now lives in Toronto, Canada. When the war started in her home city of Hargeisa, most people fled. She blames the Barre dictatorship for all of Somalia's problems and says she does not miss her country. She says she likes Canada now and feels completely at home there.

NIMCO
I AM NOT HOMESICK ANYMORE

I have been living in Toronto for eight years. I was born and raised in northwestern Somalia, in Hargeisa, the second largest city in Somalia. I came here alone, before the rest of my family arrived. Before they joined me, I stayed with relatives. Two years later the rest of my family met me in Toronto. Now I live with them. I left my country because of the civil war. There was no peace.

For the many Somalis who lived in Hargeisa, the nearest place to escape to was Ethiopia. Historically there has been war between the governments of Ethiopia and Somalia, but the civilians have always maintained good relations. Even today, Somalis and Ethiopians think of each other as brothers and sisters.

Before the civil war it was easy for people to cross the Somali-Ethiopian border from either side. It was safer for many Somalis to go to Ethiopia than to stay in Hargeisa. But as the fighting worsened, it became more difficult to approach the border. It was unsafe because the government of Somalia knew that many people were fleeing. The war was brutal. The government began to attack civilians. Government soldiers used guns and bombs to kill them.

People who wanted to cross the border into Ethiopia were often forced to walk for several days or even a few weeks to get there. No cars or buses traveled along this route. People who were trying to escape usually walked during the night and hid during the day.

I was with many people who were fleeing the civil war. Sometimes we didn't have enough food to eat or water to drink. Many people died along the way. Many people brought their elderly parents with them. Some were so ill they couldn't even walk. A lot of people lost their lives because they could not survive the hardships.

When we crossed the border, we were relieved. Many Somali refugees were already in Ethiopia. Many of them were living in camps. The day I arrived, I went with other refugees to a camp where I stayed for several months before going to North America. On the way to Canada I traveled through the United States.

A Somali boy waits alone at a refugee camp.

When I first came here, I was confused about things like culture and religion. Before I arrived, I didn't know much about Canada. When I got here, I expected to be treated equally. I also had to realize I was in a new society and I was foreign. Now I have Canadian friends and Somali ones, too. This gives me a chance to speak Somali with my Somali friends and family and English to my Canadian friends.

In Somalia I went to school until the fifth grade. I did not attend school while I was in the camp in Ethiopia.

In Somalia every subject was taught in Somali. When I came to Toronto it took me a while to

A resident of the Somalian city of Borama inspects damage to a building caused by Ethiopian bombing in 1978. Somalia waged an unsuccessful war against Ethiopia from 1976 to 1978 in an effort to regain the Ogaden territory.

get accustomed to things. In the beginning it was very hard to learn and understand English, but later it became easy. Now I can speak and understand the language well. I feel more comfortable.

I like living in Canada. I enjoy watching sports, listening to music, and going to the movies. I also like hanging out with my friends.

I am in my last year of high school. I want to go to college after I finish school. I hope to work with developing countries through the United Nations.

In Canada there are many opportunities for education and employment. Schools here offer opportunities for students to get involved in whatever they want. I like the idea of having choices. I also like being involved in community affairs, such as the Somali student association. Interacting with other Somali teens who share similar interests and experiences helps me to understand more of my own experience.

I miss my country, but I am not homesick anymore. I have not been back to Somalia. I like Canada because of the freedom and the people.

I remember Somalia as it was before the war. But now the country has changed. I hope there will be peace soon.◆

Abdi is eighteen years old and now lives in Vancouver, Canada. After leaving Somalia he went to several places to find a home. Although he has found a home in Canada, he does not have legal residency there. He often worries about his future.

ABDI
THE SIMPLER THINGS IN LIFE

7

My name is Abdi. I am from the northwestern part of Somalia. I was born in 1979 in a village called Sheik. I lived there until I was four years old. My mother had seven children including me. My father died when I was six years old. I do not have any memory of him.

I was two years old when I started to go to a special school for the study of the Koran. There I learned to recite the Koran. I also learned more about the Islamic religion. I enjoyed learning about my religion and culture with other children in my village. Every day, the *macalim* (teacher) used to teach us a new *sura* (chapter of the Koran). The next day when I came to school, I was expected to recite it. The teacher would ask me to read it without looking at the book.

When I was seven years old I left my country and moved to Virginia to stay with my sister. I went to elementary school and learned the English language. After living in Virginia for four years, I went back to northern Somalia. My mother wanted me to come back to live with her. I was happy to go back home because I missed my mother. I lived in Somalia until early 1987.

In 1987 things started to deteriorate. Troops were visible everywhere. People were not allowed to walk the streets at night. We were forced to live like we were under house arrest—we were prisoners in our own homes. My family decided to leave for Mogadishu, where things were a little better. While I was living there, I went to an English-language school run by Indians since I knew English. I wanted to keep up my English in case I had to go back to the United States.

Even though the political situation was at its lowest point, I liked how it brought people together. I felt that people were closer and looked after each other. For example, families and friends checked on each other a lot. I looked forward to the end of the day, when all the kids in my neighborhood would gather and tell stories, play games, or have singing contests. The simpler things in life were appreciated more in Somalia. I get nostalgic when I hear the songs we used to sing. There were also poems that criticized the political situation.

Demonstrators of several opposing political groups parade through the streets of Mogadishu to celebrate Somalia's independence from colonial rule in 1960.

In 1990, things got really bad. Gunshots could be heard all the time. People started forming gangs. The city was totally unstable. One night, my cousin and I were upstairs in our house, sitting on the balcony. As we were talking, we saw a man walking below. He was staring at us. Then my cousin told him to stop staring at us. We continued to talk. We thought he was gone, but he suddenly came out of a corner and started to shoot at us. We ran inside the house to hide. Everybody got scared and kept quiet. This was a scary moment. This was my closest encounter with guns. I knew that nowhere was safe.

I finally left Mogadishu in 1992 and went to Kismayu. I stayed there for four months in a house with no roof or windows. Still, I was among the lucky ones. Many people who came could not find anyplace to stay. Then I went to Amuume, a town in Kenya close to the Somali border.

I stayed in Kenya for a couple of months. I collected money from relatives to go to Cairo, Egypt, and from there I flew to Virginia. I stayed with my sister again. But it was hard because I did not have any immigration papers in the United States. I heard that Canada was accepting many Somali refugees, so I decided to go there.

The only person I knew in Canada was my nephew, who lived in Vancouver. I went to live with him.

When I first came to Canada I did not like it. It was too cold. I also missed my family, who were scattered around the world. The only news I heard about Somalia was from television.

To cope as a teenager and a refugee was difficult for me. Then I met other Somali teens who had similar experiences, which was comforting for me. I also started to go to school.

I began writing poems about my experience and my perception of the world. Poetry became the only way I could express myself—it is a coping mechanism.

A few weeks after I came here I began filing my legal papers. I was accepted as a refugee but never got my residency. This is why I cannot go to college—it is very expensive for non-residents to go to college in Canada. Now I have been here for five years.

I am very active in the Somali community. I want to help the Somali youth. Currently, I work for a settlement agency as a case worker. Someday, I will be able to earn my college degree. Then I will be able to do even more for the Somali youth who have gone through hard times like I have.◆

Glossary

chaos A confusing and unpredictable situation.

clan A group of people tracing descent from a common ancestor.

colonial power A foreign power that rules over a nation or a territory.

diya Money paid by a person who has injured or killed another person.

Id A month of celebration in the Islamic religion.

infrastructure A country's system of public works (roads, bridges, and electricity, for example).

Islam A religion that holds that Allah is the one God. Its teachings are found in the Koran, which Muslims believe was revealed to Muhammad.

National Assembly Political body in Somalia similar to the U.S. Congress.

nomad A person who has no fixed residence and wanders the countryside.

parochial Related to a church parish.

Ramadan Fasting month of the year in the Islamic religion.

refugee Person who flees his or her country because of war or persecution.

For Further Reading

Fox, Mary Virginia. *Somalia*. New York: Children's
    Press, 1996.
Godbeer, Deadre. *Somalia*. New York: Chelsea
    House, 1988.
Hassig, Susan M. *Somalia*. North Bellmore, NY:
    Marshall Cavendish, 1997.
Matthews, Jo. *I Remember Somalia*. Austin, TX:
    Raintree Steck-Vaughn, 1995.
Ricciuti, Edward R. *Somalia: A Crisis of Famine
    and War*. Brookfield, CT: Millbrook Press,
    1993.
Sheik-'Abdi, 'Abdi ('Abdi 'Abdulqadir). *Somali
    Folktales*. 1st ed. Macomb, IL: Dr. Leisure,
    1993.